Recycling EARTH'S Resources

Barbara L. Webb

Rourke
Educational Media
rourkeeducationalmedia.com

www.rourkeeducationalmedia.com

PHOTO CREDITS: Cover, Page 11: © mark wragg; Title Page: © Yunis Arakon; Page 4: © Andrei Harwell, © Sze Kit Poon; Page 5: © Borut Trdina, © Lew Robertson; Page 6: © Serhiy Zavalnyuk; Page 7: © Iakov Kalinin; Page 9, 10: © Jacom Stephens; Page 11: © mark wragg, © Zentilia; Page 12: © Jani Bryson; Page 13: © Claude Dagenais; Page 14: © Wei Shein Yap; Page 15: © Nick White, © manuel velasco; Page 16: © Philip Danze; Page 17: © Sebastien Cote; Page 18: © Franky De Meyer; Page 19: © carolecastelli; Page 21: © ranplett

Edited by Kelli L. Hicks

Cover and Interior design by Tara Raymo

Library of Congress Cataloging-in-Publication Data

Webb, Barbara L.
  Recycling earth's resources / Barbara L. Webb.
    p. cm. -- (Green earth science)
  Includes bibliographical references and index.
  ISBN 978-1-61590-299-6 (Hard Cover) (alk. paper)
  ISBN 978-1-61590-538-6 (Soft Cover)
  1. Recycling (Waste, etc.)--United States--Juvenile literature. 2. Refuse and refuse disposal--United States--Juvenile literature. I. Title.
  TD794.5.W3829 2011
  363.72'82--dc22
                                        2010009867

Rourke Educational Media
Printed in the United States of America, North Mankato, Minnesota

rourkeeducationalmedia.com

customerservice@rourkeeducationalmedia.com • PO Box 643328 Vero Beach, Florida 32964

Table of Contents

Earth's Resources

The Earth gives us many **resources**.

We use water for drinking and washing.

We use **metals** to make forks and knives.

We use sand
to make glass.

We use trees to
make paper.

We use other
plants for food.

The Earth makes resources slowly.

The Earth takes a long time to make trees and a very long time to make metal. The Earth does not make any more water at all.

Shovels that mine ore can hold up to 85 tons (77 metric tons) of rock!

Recycling Earth's Resources

We will use up Earth's resources too quickly if we throw all of our used things in the trash. Our trash will start to take up too much space.

What else can we do with our used resources?

8

We can **recycle** them! Recycling makes
something new out of something old.

This symbol means recycle. You will see it on the bottom of things you can recycle and on cans or bins that collect things to be recycled.

How Recycling Works

The metal, paper, glass, and plastic you put into a recycling bin goes to a recycling center.

Workers at the recycling center sort things into different piles. We recycle different resources in different ways.

We squash up old paper and roll it out
into new paper.

We melt metal cans and glass bottles to make new ones.

We can even turn our leftover food into rich dirt that helps new plants grow.

This rich dirt is called **compost**.

We clean and recycle our water. Used water from our toilets and sinks follows the pipes to the water treatment plant.

The water treatment plant cleans the water and puts it back out into our lakes and rivers.

Recycling Is Smart

If we recycle, we will still have Earth's resources to use tomorrow. Our trash will take up less space.

Try This

Ask a grown-up to help you do this paper recycling project. Never try to use a blender by yourself. Be safe!

1. Tear up paper into small squares.
2. Soak the paper in water overnight.
3. Measure one part of the paper in a blender with two parts water.
4. Blend the paper.
5. Staple a window screen to cover a picture frame.
6. Fill a tub with two inches (five centimeters) of water and add the paper.
7. Scoop up the paper with your frame and shake it to drain the water off.
8. Cover your paper with a piece of square felt and dry it with a paper towel.
9. Flip the screen over onto a cookie sheet and tap or peel the paper off.
10. Let your paper dry. Flatten it with a large book.
11. You have recycled paper!

Glossary

compost (KOM-pohst): a mixture of rotted leaves, vegetables, plants, and worm droppings that can be added to garden soil

metals (MET-uhlz): chemical matters that are usually hard, shiny, and good conductors of electricity

recycle (ree-SYE-kuhl): to process old materials like paper, plastic, and glass so that they can be used to make new things

resources (REE-sours-ez): natural things we can use

Index

Websites

www.kidsrecyclingzone.com

www.recycleguys.org

yucky.discovery.com/flash/worm/pg000104.html

www.epa.gov/safewater/kids/kids_k-3.html

About the Author

Barbara Webb lives in Chicago, Illinois. She does not mind carrying her recycling bin down eight floors to dump it in the bigger recycling bin. She loves writing books about things kids are curious about, like presidents, trees, and recycling!